# HIV & AIDS, Communication, and Secondary Education in Kenya

## Zapf Chancery Tertiary Level Publications

*A Guide to Academic Writing* by C. B. Peter (1994)

*Africa in the 21st Century* by Eric M. Aseka (1996)

*Women in Development* by Egara Kabaji (1997)

*Introducing Social Science: A Guidebook* by J. H. van Doorne (2000)

*Elementary Statistics* by J. H. van Doorne (2001)

*Iteso Survival Rites on the Birth of Twins* by Festus B. Omusolo (2001)

*The Church in the New Millennium: Three Studies in the Acts of the Apostles* by John Stott (2002)

*Introduction to Philosophy in an African Perspective* by Cletus N.Chukwu (2002)

*Participatory Monitoring and Evaluation* by Francis W. Mulwa and Simon N. Nguluu (2003)

*Applied Ethics and HIV/AIDS in Africa* by Cletus N. Chukwu (2003)

*For God and Humanity: 100 Years of St. Paul's United Theological College* Edited by Emily Onyango (2003)

*Establishing and Managing School Libraries and Resource Centres* by Margaret Makenzi and Raymond Ongus (2003)

*Introduction to the Study of Religion* by Nehemiah Nyaundi (2003)

*A Guest in God's World: Memories of Madagascar* by Patricia McGregor (2004)

*Introduction to Critical Thinking* by J. Kahiga Kiruki (2004)

*Theological Education in Contemporary Africa* edited by GrantLeMarquand and Joseph D. Galgalo (2004)

*Looking Religion in the Eye* edited by Kennedy Onkware (2004)

*Computer Programming: Theory and Practice* by Gerald Injendi (2005)

*Demystifying Participatory Development* by Francis W. Mulwa (2005)

*Music Education in Kenya: A Historical Perspective* by Hellen A. Odwar (2005)

*Into the Sunshine: Integrating HIV/AIDS into Ethics Curriculum* Edited by Charles Klagba and C. B. Peter (2005)

*Integrating HIV/AIDS into Ethics Curriculum: Suggested Modules* Edited by Charles Klagba (2005)

*Dying Voice (An Anthropological Novel)* by Andrew K. Tanui (2006)

*Participatory Learning and Action (PLA): A Guide to Best Practice* by Enoch Harun Opuka (2006)

*Science and Human Values: Essays in Science, Religion, and Modern Ethical Issues* edited by Nehemiah Nyaundi and Kennedy Onkware (2006)

*Understanding Adolescent Behaviour* by Daniel Kasomo (2006)

*Students' Handbook for Guidance and Counselling* by Daniel Kasomo (2007)

*BusinessOrganization and Management: Questions and Answers* by Musa O. Nyakora (2007)

*Auditing Priniples: A Stuents' Handbook* by Musa O. Nyakora (2007)

*The Concept of Botho and HIV/AIDS in Botswana* edite by Joseph B. R. Gaie and Sana K. MMolai (2007)

*Captive of Fate: A Novel* by Ketty Arucy (2007)

*A Guide to Ethics* by Joseph Njino (2008)

(Continued after Bibliography)

# HIV & AIDS, Communication, and Secondary Education in Kenya

**Ndeti Ndati**

**Lecturer, St. Paul's University, Limuru, Kenya**

*Zapf Chancery*
**Eldoret, Kenya**

First Published 2011
©Ndeti Ndati
*All rights reserved.*

*Cover Concept and Design*
C. B. Peter

*Associate Designer and Typesetter*
Nancy Njeri

*Copyediting*
C. B. Peter

*Editor and Publishing Consultant*
C. B. Peter

*Printed by*
Kijabe Printing Press,
P. O. Box 40,
Kijabe.

*Published by*

Zapf Chancery Research Consultants and Publishers,
P. O. Box 4988,
Eldoret, Kenya.
Email: zapfchancerykenya@yahoo.co.uk
Mobile: 0721-222 311

ISBN 978-9966-7341-9-8

*To my loving wife Jackie, my twin sons Ndeto and Mutinda, and my daughter Ndanu.*

# Acknowledgements

My sincere gratitude goes to Ms. Wambui Kiai and Mr. Edwin Nyutho who supervised me during my MA research work. I feel humbled by their timely advice, guidance and encouragement. I wouldn't have succeeded without them.

My appreciation also goes to Dr. Joseph Mbindyo who guided me through the initial stages of this research.

I am also grateful to Anne Mumo and Bernard Kamanda who worked tirelessly in typing the entire document. Their commitment, skill, patience and great sense of responsibility were just incredible.

I sincerely appreciate the work of Rev. C. B. Peter, my editorial consultant, whose encouragement and scholarly direction resulted in the publication of this book.

My special thanks go to my wife Jackie, for her continued love, prayers and encouragement which gave me the drive to complete this book.

To you all I am deeply indebted.
*May God bless you!*

# List of Abbreviations and Acronyms

| | | |
|---|---|---|
| **AAWORD** | : | Association of African Women for Research and Development |
| **AIDS** | : | Acquired Immune Deficiency Syndrome |
| **AIDSCAP** | : | AIDS Control and Prevention |
| **ANC** | : | Ante-Natal Clinic |
| **CBS** | : | Central Bureau of Statistics |
| **CDC** | : | Centres for Disease Control |
| **GOK** | : | Government of Kenya |
| **HIV** | : | Human Immunodeficiency Virus |
| **KIE** | : | Kenya Institute of Education |
| **KNHACS** | : | Kenya National HIV & AIDS Communication Strategy |
| **LDCs** | : | Least Developed Countries |
| **MOH** | : | Ministry of Health |
| **NACC** | : | National Aids Control Council |

| | | |
|---|---|---|
| **NASCOP** | : | National AIDS and STD Control Programme |
| **NGOs** | : | Non-Governmental Organizations |
| **STD** | : | Sexually Transmitted Diseases |
| **UN** | : | United Nations |
| **UNAIDS** | : | United Nations Programme on HIV & AIDS |
| **UNESCO** | : | United Nations Educational, Scientific and Cultural Organization. |
| **UNICEF** | : | United Nations International Children's Education Fund |
| **VCT** | : | Voluntary Counselling and Testing |
| **WHO** | : | World Health Organization |
| **WHO/GPA** | : | World Health Organization's Global Programme on AIDS |

# CHAPTER ONE

# Introduction

## Background

Acquired Immune Deficiency Syndrome (AIDS) is a problem affecting all countries worldwide. By the beginning of year 2000, the United Nations Programme on HIV & AIDS (UNAIDS) and the World Health Organization (WHO) estimated that over 34 million people were infected with HIV, while 13 million people around the world had died of AIDS. Today, although one in every 100 adults in the sexually active age bracket (15-49) is living with HIV, only a tiny fraction knows about their infections (NACC, 2000).

HIV infections are concentrated in the least developed countries (LDCs), with 89 per cent of the people living with HIV & AIDS in Sub-Saharan Africa and Asia. Of all people living with HIV & AIDS in the world (34 million), over two thirds (22 million), live in Africa. It is estimated that 87% of children living with HIV & AIDS in the world also live in Africa (NACC, 2000).

Unlike other medical conditions, HIV & AIDS is as much a social issue as a medical problem. Primarily transmitted through one of the commonest human activities, sexual intercourse, it brings protracted illness and early death to men and women in the prime of their lives, kills new-born children and leaves their older brothers and sisters in emotional and physical misery. The epidemic feeds on the deep divisions within our societies – illiteracy, ignorance, poverty and inequality between the sexes – and deepens those divisions by making our communities poorer.

In all but a few countries, the response to AIDS has been inadequate. Millions of men and women who are fully aware of the threat of HIV are unwilling or unable to protect themselves and their partners. Religious and political leaders have failed to understand the extent and the complex nature of the epidemic and have failed to provide the leadership required to protect their citizens' lives and livelihoods. And all too often the reaction toward those affected by the disease has been of fear, hatred and contempt instead of the compassion and assistance that they and the society as a whole require.

Acquired Immune Deficiency Syndrome (AIDS) is a tragedy of devastating proportions in Kenya. The lives of infected individuals, their families and communities, the companies and agencies they work for, and the society as a whole are all affected by HIV & AIDS pandemic. It is estimated that by June 2000, 1.5 million people in Kenya had died of AIDS since the early 1980s when the epidemic started. The main modes of transmission of HIV are sexual contact, mother-to-child transmission and contact with blood.

The National AIDS Control Council (NACC) estimates that the national HIV prevalence rose from 5.3 per cent in 1990 to 13.1 per cent in 1999. Prevalence is generally higher in urban areas, with an average of 16-17 per cent than in rural areas, with an average of 11-12 percent.

HIV & AIDS is difficult to combat because of the rising trend of poverty, the unpredictable progress of HIV, and the underlying behavioural factors. Lack of resources to finance implementation of cost-effective interventions due to the prevailing weak economic performance is a major source of ongoing concern for Kenya.

The present study seeks to evaluate communication strategies related to HIV & AIDS for adolescents in secondary schools. Studies indicate that the highest proportion of AIDS cases are between 14-39 years and that adolescents are becoming sexually active at a younger age, (Nduati et al, 1996) meaning that the risk of AIDS is higher among this group. Further, there is concern about the fact that the reported cases do not represent the real picture of the magnitude of infection as some people are unable or unwilling to seek medical care or to go for testing.

Adolescence is defined by WHO as the age between 15-24 years. The Centre for Disease Control (CDC) defines it as 13-19 years, while the American Academy of Paediatrics and Society for Adolescent Medicine define it as 13-31 years (Nduati et al, 1996). According to *Oxford Advanced Learners Dictionary*, an adolescent is a young person between childhood and adulthood (ages 13-17). For the purpose of my study, 13 to 17 years is the age bracket to be considered as adolescence.

Irresponsible adolescent sexuality, compounded with the phenomenon of HIV & AIDS, has brought about many adverse outcomes that include unwanted pregnancies, disrupted education, reduced employment opportunities, low income, unstable marriages, sexually transmitted diseases, and health and development risks for the children of adolescents, curtailed life, early widowhood and more orphans. My concern for adolescence in the present study is for two reasons: first, the 5-15 years age group is relatively free of HIV & AIDS, and secondly, it is indicated from epidemiological data that two out of every three HIV infected individuals acquire infection during adolescence (WHO/GPA). Thus, the adolescents and youth need to be targeted specifically so that they remain free of HIV infection.

Youths below 15 years of age comprise 50 per cent of the total Kenyan population. Epidemiological data has demonstrated that the period 5-15 years is relatively free of HIV infection and the term "window of hope" has been coined for this age-set. Governments have been targeting this group of young people for information dissemination and training in methods of preventing HIV & AIDS.

After the age of 15 years, HIV and other sexually transmitted diseases have been shown to increase rapidly in adolescents. This increase in HIV & AIDS and STDs correspond to initiation of sexual activity. Sexually transmitted diseases have been a significant co-factor in the transmission of HIV & AIDS.

Adolescents are reared in the nurturing units of the family and the clan. These units set the spiritual, emotional and physical identity of the youth. The family is very important in setting the limits for behaviour. Families that have a mutual closeness are characterised by youth who defer their sexuality (Grant, 1988 in Nduati et al, 1996). However, lack of information and barriers in communication because of socially determined taboos, limits parents' ability to counsel the adolescents. The second barrier is the fact that the older adolescents are influenced more by their peers than by their parents (Nduati, et al, 1996). Young people seek out peer groups in which they feel that their potential is fulfilled. These groups may have tremendous impact on the youth behaviour.

The magnitude and impact of HIV & AIDS in Kenya is not just a major public health problem development challenge but is increasingly creating severe negative socio-economic impact. The realisation that Kenya is losing about 350 of its people daily to HIV & AIDS has led the government to declare HIV & AIDS, a National Disaster. More than one million people have developed AIDS and died since 1984, leaving behind close to one million orphans. In 1999, about two million Kenyans were living with HIV. In one year alone, close to 200,000 new HIV infections occur in the country and about seventy three per cent of those already infected live in rural areas. AIDS-prevalence has been reported in every district in Kenya.

While a cure or vaccine remains elusive, AIDS remains the biggest challenge to the government because of its current and future impact on Kenya's economic growth. This is why former President Daniel Arap Moi, while addressing members of Parliament in Mombasa on 25th November, 1999, declared AIDS a National Disaster stating:

> Aids is not just a serious threat to our very social and economic development, it is a real threat to our very existence … AIDS has reduced many families to the status of beggars … no family in Kenya remains untouched by the suffering and death caused by AIDS… the real solution of the spread of AIDS lies with each and every one of us.

There are no easy answers when it comes to deciding how to teach adolescents about AIDS, and persuading them to protect themselves from AIDS is an even greater challenge. Adolescents often perceive themselves to be invulnerable, and most young people perceive AIDS to be only a remote possibility. This perception is strengthened by the fact that they have rarely been taught to take responsibility for their health.

A significant shift which is relevant to AIDS communication and adolescents is that audiences are no longer viewed as being passive and recipient to any messages as determined by imitators of various projects and programmes. In order to be able to develop programmes that address change and behaviour in adolescents it is important to have an understanding of the youth, culture surrounding sexuality, their sources of information and the factors that influence them (Nduati, et al; 1996).

Factors that affect human and social behaviour, such as poverty, discrimination, and disenfranchisement have to be addressed on a global basis if HIV & AIDS epidemic is to be controlled. AIDS has revealed the gaps in the understanding of how human behaviour is motivated and how it can be changed.

## Problem Statement

The present study sought to examine the impact of HIV & AIDS communication strategies for adolescents. It was, specifically, a case study of the HIV & AIDS Education Programme in Kenya's selected secondary schools.

The need to focus on the HIV & AIDS Education programme was necessitated by such factors as the desperate situation brought about by the rising prevalence rate of HIV & AIDS, which calls for an urgent analysis of the factors that constrain behaviour change. Adolescents have also been found to comprise the highest percentage of the infections in addition to facing a multiplicity of risks because of their vulnerability.

In a situation where the cure for AIDS has remained elusive, preventive efforts to further check the spread of HIV & AIDS has become the method of choice for stakeholders working in this particular field.

Young people comprise almost 60 percent of the total population in Kenya and have correctly been described as the window of hope in the fight against the HIV & AIDS pandemic.

There is no single confirmed cause for the spread of AIDS. Hence there is no single means of prevention. AIDS requires a multimethod and multi-channel intervention guided by prior theory and research in a variety of disciplines, one of which is communication, indeed a pivotal discipline. With AIDS there is greater urgency to discover factors that produce high-risk behaviour. Since, there is no cure for AIDS at this time; prevention and care are our only strategies in our battle against the pandemic. One of our main challenges is the development of persuasive interventions for use through both mass media and interpersonal communication channels.

Adolescents constitute a particularly important and challenging target for AIDS prevention interventions. Several factors increase the probability of AIDS-risky behaviour among the adolescents: a sense of vulnerability, sexual exploration and experimentation, dysfunctional beliefs and attitudes towards health care services and reliance on peer networks rather reliable sources of information.

Young people are much more vulnerable to HIV & AIDS than are older people. Because their social, emotional and psychological development is incomplete, young people tend to experiment with risky behaviour, often caring little about the danger. In fact, risky sexual behaviour is often part of a larger pattern of adolescent behaviour, including alcohol and drug abuse, delinquency and rebellion against the authority.

A number of reasons explain why adolescents indulge in high risk sex. Adolescents become involved in sex probably for monetary gains. Poverty may explain their limited knowledge and involvement in high risk sexual encounters. There are also gender differences to explain why adolescents indulge in sex. Boys have to demonstrate their dominance over girls and hence are aggressive in seducing them. Furthermore, both boys and girls indulge in sex with multiple partners to satisfy the sexual desire and fantasy for change. Some young men want to prove they are "real men" and feel great and famous by having many partners (Nduati et al, 1996).

The general knowledge of AIDS and its recognition as a life-threat to youth is a necessary prerequisite to behaviour change. The war on AIDS will require a concerted effort on every front. As with other adolescent health issues, the fight against AIDS is being fought as a multi-channel, multi-method and a multi-disciplinary fight.

The present study derives from the concern over increase in HIV & AIDS prevalence among adolescents in spite of efforts to control it. Based on the problem stated, the study is an evaluation of the AIDS education programme for adolescents in Kenya's selected Secondary schools.

## Objective of the Study

The objective of the present study was to investigate the levels of awareness, knowledge and information the youth have gained through AIDS education programmes in some secondary schools in Kenya.

## Justification of the Study

STIs including HIV are common among adolescents aged between 15 and 24 years, and it has been estimated that half of all HIV infections have occurred among people aged less than 25 years, which means that adolescents are at the greatest risk (WHO, 1995).

Adolescents attain puberty early and marry late, and are therefore more likely to engage in pre-marital sex than members of their parents' generation were. Vulnerability to HIV is systematically patterned to make some young people more likely to be infected than others.

Given the significant numbers of young people living in the Less Developed Countries (LDCs) seriously affected by the epidemic, it is crucial that intervention is undertaken to ensure that they are able to protect themselves.

Therefore, there is need for the provision of information and resources as well as promoting a climate, which understands young people and their sexual health needs. Such interventions include the school-based programmes that comprise the provision of factual information through posters, songs, poetry and theatre. Another intervention is the HIV & AIDS Education programme taught in schools.

The above needs justified the present study. The results of the study could benefit the government in establishing whether the HIV & AIDS Education programme is a success or otherwise. The study will also contribute significantly in determining the levels of HIV & AIDS awareness among the youth in high schools.

The findings of this study could contribute to policy making and implementation for effective control of HIV & AIDS among the youth.

## Scope of the Study

Although there are many interventions targeting the youth, and with the express objective of preventing the transmission of HIV & AIDS, the present study focussed on only one intervention – AIDS education intervention in schools.

Due to limitations of time and finances, the present study was conducted in Nairobi over a duration of three (3) months.

## Definition of Terms

Following are definition of terms that I have used frequently in the present book.

- *AIDS*: Acquired Immune Deficiency Syndrome: A cluster of medical conditions often referred to as opportunistic infections for which, to date, there is no cure.
- *Impact*: It means strong impression or effect on somebody.
- *HIV*: Human Immunodeficiency Virus. This virus weakens the body's immune system, ultimately causing AIDS.

- *Education*: A system of training and instruction, especially of children and young people in schools, designed to give knowledge and develop skills.
- *Programme*: A plan of what is intended to be done. A programmed course is an educational course in which the material to be learnt is presented in small, carefully graded amounts.
- *Communication*: A process of transmission of modes of thinking, feeling, and behaving from one person (or persons) to another person (or persons). An important goal of communication is persuasion and feedback.
- *Strategy*: It means a plan or policy designed for a particular purpose.
- *Intervention*: An instance of becoming involved in a situation either to make something to happen, or to prevent something from happening.
- *Adolescent*: A young person aged between childhood and adulthood, roughly between the ages of 13 and 17.
- *School*: An institution for educating children, either primary or secondary

# CHAPTER TWO

# The HIV & AIDS Regime: An Overview

## Introduction

In the last 20 years, HIV & AIDS has evolved into a global pandemic. Sub-Saharan Africa has borne the brunt of this pandemic because of the socio-economic, political and cultural factors that provide fertile grounds for an explosion of infections. Poverty and illiteracy have contributed by limiting access to information and ability to modify lifestyles in order to reduce the risk of infection. Poverty has resulted in African governments being unable to provide sufficient health care and as a result sexually transmitted diseases which fuel HIV & AIDS spread are rampant. Poverty, lack of employment and male migration to urban centres have made it difficult for African families to hold together as a unit, thus rendering them less able to nurture their offspring and at the same time exposing them to lifestyles that increase the risk of HIV & AIDS.

There is still no cure for HIV & AIDS and prevention is the mainstay of controlling the epidemic.

The youth need culturally sensitive programs that provide an explicit and honest explanation to sexuality, gender issues, safer sexual practices STDs and HIV, safer motherhood, and family planning. All potential behavioural change including abstinence or condom use should be taught to the youth.

In the new AIDS Education Syllabus for schools and colleges developed by the Kenya Institute of Education, culture has been presented as an area of study. In *"Bloom or Doom: Your choice,"* a resource book for teaching secondary school students, the chapter on culture is very explicit. The author looks at culture as a dynamic process which determines how, where and why we live the way we do. Our culture reflects what we have inherited from our ancestors and how we have adapted to it in our current situation.

As our lifestyle changes, so do our needs. Our traditional cultural practices had a role for each member of the society. Just like the traditional cultures saw the need for identifying suitable leisure activities for youth, so do modern cultures. Most communities have activities for members to participate during leisure time. These activities are positively geared to spiritually, physically and socially benefit us. They are also trouble free and carefully planned to avoid situations that expose us

Since culture keeps changing, the school curriculum also changes. Our culture has changed significantly since the onset of HIV & AIDS. This has made it necessary to teach the youth about HIV & AIDS in order to create awareness on how some of the cultural practices can be a means of transmitting HIV & AIDS. This will then help in controlling the spread of HIV & AIDS. In any discussion of HIV & AIDS and behaviour, the centrality of culture cannot be ignored. Clearly, because the specific interest lies in the change of behaviour which is governed by attitude and levels of knowledge, special concern and analysis of culture must be given in HIV & AIDS programs.

Certain aspects of culture are pertinent in any deliberation on communication on HIV & AIDS and behaviour. The basic consideration is that: "Culture constitutes the very matrix within which people formulate their ideas, within which they carry out their activities" (Borofsky in Nduati, et al, 1996).

A comprehensive understanding of cultural dynamics and their impact on behavioural relationships and how this impacts on the spread of HIV & AIDS is a necessity.

In the diverse African cultures, the passage from childhood into adulthood was marked with a variety of rites and specific customs. Customs are important building blocks for each culture. Each of the African countries has had a diversity of cultures and it's only in the 20th century that a process of developing a national culture has emerged. Culture is based on sets of customary laws that are different from the written laws. Customary laws define the transition from childhood to adulthood, and prescribe behaviours and roles that newly initiated adults should take (Balmer 1994 in Nduati, et al; 1996).

In the latter part of the 20th century, the adolescent in Africa has been exposed to political change as countries experienced a transition from colonialism to independence, civil strife, dictatorship, military coups, wars and internal displacement. In the late 80s, and beyond, HIV & AIDS has decimated families and led to the phenomenon of child-headed households. At the same time, most African countries have been in economic crises for several years and African population has experienced poverty, which affect the adolescents in their spheres such as education and meeting of their basic needs.

The influence of Westernization has led to change in social interaction and social patterns, which in turn has resulted into lack of common responsibility on social issues. For instance, because of the absence of a clear definition of who will undertake sex education for adolescents, the confusion created by the cultural vacuum has hampered communities and governments from developing a clear policy. The prevailing political, cultural, economic and social turmoil in Africa has resulted in the emergence of the disempowered and demoralized adult society, which is complacent or helpless when faced with handling the issue of adolescent development, or with the HIV & AIDS epidemic (Nduati, et al, 1996).

Over the last decade, HIV & AIDS has become the world's most devastating epidemic, particularly in developing countries, where many governments have declared it an emergency. Worldwide, it is estimated that about 22 million people have died of AIDS; 36 million are currently infected with HIV, the virus that causes AIDS; and out of these, approximately 70% live in Sub-Saharan Africa (NASCOP, 2001).

The first AIDS case in Kenya was reported in the mid-1980s, and by 1995, 63,179 cases had been reported. Presently, it is estimated that about 2.2 million Kenyans are infected with HIV & AIDS, while 1.5 million Kenyans have already died from AIDS related illnesses. In Kenya, most people contract HIV through unprotected sexual contact, while a significant proportion of mothers pass the virus to the child during pregnancy, labour and delivery or through breastfeeding. It is also estimated that about 5 to 10% of infections in developing countries like Kenya is acquired through blood transfusion (NACC, 2001).

In the early years of the epidemic, programme managers often lacked information on the mode of transmission and the interventions necessary to slow down the spread of this deadly virus. In more recent years knowledge about the virus has grown tremendously, making it easier to monitor the trends while measuring the impact of various interventions.

The government is committed to winning the battle against HIV and AIDS. On 25th November, 1999 the then President Daniel Arap Moi declared AIDS a national disaster. Subsequently, the government mobilized additional resources and established a National AIDS Control Council to advocate, strengthen, and coordinate the multi-sectoral response to contain the spread of the HIV virus and mitigate the impact of AIDS.

Against the reality of a fast-growing epidemic and prohibitive cost of antiretroviral drugs, most efforts are aimed at prevention through increasing awareness about the risk of transmission of HIV and promoting positive behaviour change. This includes promoting abstinence before marriage and faithfulness to one partner, and the availability and use of condoms by those who are sexually active and at the risk of spreading or contracting HIV. Establishment of Voluntary Counselling and testing (VCT) centres, early diagnosis and treatment of sexually transmitted diseases and tuberculosis, provision of services to prevent mother-to-child transmission, and maintaining safe blood supply and equipment at health centres are other important interventions.

Since there is no cure for AIDS, this disease threatens the social and economic future of the country. However, this threat can be overcome; its outcome is not inevitable. If we act now, there is much we can do to slow the spread of HIV and reduce its negative impact on development. In his foreword to the Kenya National HIV & AIDS strategic plan, the then President, Daniel Arap Moi declared, "The fight against AIDS is a war we must win!" (NACC, 2000).

The major mode of transmission of HIV in Kenya is through sexual intercourse. The epidemic primarily affects young working age, sexually active adults – the people between the ages 15 and 50. Both women and men become infected in similar numbers, but women tend to become infected at a younger age than men, reflecting the biological and social vulnerability of teenage women.

An accurate estimation of HIV prevalence is necessary to assess the scope of the AIDS epidemic in Kenya and track trends over time. In Kenya, as in most of Sub-Saharan Africa, national HIV prevalence estimates have been derived primarily from sentinel surveillance in pregnant women. Currently, the national sentinel surveillance system consists of 42 clinics in government and mission health facilities selected to represent the different groups, regions and rural urban populations in the country. For three months each year since 1990, pregnant women registering their 1st visit to the Ante-Natal Clinic (ANC) are anonymously tested for HIV and the results analysed by the National AIDS & STD Control Programme (NASCOP, 2003].

Despite data which shows that awareness of HIV & AIDS with the public is high and there is significant knowledge about HIV/AIDS, there is no concomitant change of behaviour. (NACC, 2001) This statement remains true as long as we are referring to the behaviour of older, sexually active, adolescents and adults. However, when we consider the vast majority of younger adolescents who should be the subject of greater focus, then we begin to appreciate the need for more innovative communication for prevention, that address this group before they become sexually active.

Why does adolescence increase vulnerability to HIV & AIDS? Adolescence is a period of unpredictable behaviour. Lacking the judgement that comes with experience, adolescents cannot appreciate the adverse consequences of their actions.

The risks of HIV & AIDS may be particularly hard for young people to grasp. Because HIV has a long incubation period, a person's risky behaviour may not manifest immediate consequences. At the same time, the potential social costs to a young person of preventing HIV infection – including loss of the relationship, loss of trust, and loss of peer acceptance – can be too high a price for most adolescents to bear. Moreover, many young people are unaware of what constitutes risky sexual behaviour.

Even if they appreciate the risks for HIV & AIDS in general, many adolescents do not seem to think that they themselves can be vulnerable to the risk of contracting HIV. Even when they know the risk, some young people may ignore it. Young women may engage intentionally in risky sexual behaviour especially in cultures where marriage is highly valued and a woman's status depends on finding a husband and having children. In some parts of Cameroon, competition for eligible men is keen. Thus young women who face the threat of being displaced by other girlfriends may engage in unprotected sexual intercourse to bolster their chances of finding husbands. In parts of Asia, young women may become sex workers because they receive higher pay than in many other occupations.

For many adolescents, experimenting with tobacco, alcohol, sex and drugs are rites of passage. The propensity to take risks applies to all sorts of risks. In Tanzania, for example, youth aged 16 to 24 who smoke, and drink alcohol are four times more likely than others in that age to have multiple sex partners (retrieved from http// www.jhuccp.org). In Kenya, the single most important predictor of sexual activity among adolescent women is using alcohol, drugs or tobacco.

The HIV & AIDS pandemic in Sub-Saharan African countries is a clear threat, which demands urgent attention. An integrated approach using all relevant means and channels in society is required to confront the threat, and the use of communication media is especially important in this respect. Bringing about positive results in the efforts to stem the prevalence of HIV & AIDS depends, among other things, on the existence of an informed public that is sensitive to the causes, spread and prevention of the epidemic.

Communication holds the key to containing HIV transmission and coping with the effects of the AIDS pandemic. However, over the last 20 years, communication has failed to confront and contain HIV/AIDS, and in this period, it has killed more than 20 million worldwide. In 2002, more than 3 million died from AIDS (Panos Report, 2003).

In *Missing the Message? 20 years of learning from HIV & AIDS*, a report issued for World AIDS Day, Panos evaluated HIV & AIDS communication data and argued that it is time for nothing less than a fundamental reappraisal of HIV communication strategies.

Though it is widely reported that the strength and vision of national political leadership in the cases of Uganda, Senegal, Thailand and Brazil have been crucial to successfully combating HIV & AIDS, those successes also have other lesser known ingredients such as open public debate. This open debate, with local, public participation and ownership is crucial.

Drawing on the UNAIDS Communication Framework for HIV & AIDS and the Rockefeller Foundation Communication for Social Change Network, the report identifies that most current theories of HIV communication programming have many weaknesses including:

- The assumption that decisions about HIV & AIDS prevention are based on rational, volitional thinking with no regard to true-to-life emotional responses to engaging in sex.

- The focus on condom promotion to the exclusion of the need to address the importance and centrality of social contexts, including government policy, socio-economic status, culture, gender relations, and spirituality.

Approaches should move from putting out messages to fostering an environment where the voice of the most affected by the epidemic can be heard. This shift from message to voice is much more effective. While HIV & AIDS information and key health message remain crucial, it is important to look beyond these messages – no matter how empowering and context-sensitive they might be – and help to develop environments where vibrant and internally derived dialogue can flourish.

### Effects of HIV Infection and AIDS

An individual gets affected by HIV & AIDS both physically and psychologically. As the HIV infection gradually leads to full blown AIDS, the infected person experiences the social stigma that is associated with the disease. His or her weakened condition denies him or her opportunity to work and earn a living. This leads to economic hardships due to the loss in earnings. This is especially difficult for such a person because he or she needs money for medical care arising from the opportunistic infections that often afflict persons suffering from AIDS. These people also need to maintain a balanced diet, which in some cases can be very expensive.

The loss of earnings does not only affect the infected person. It also affects the members of his or her family, especially if he or she is a parent or sole bread earner. Since individual families do not live in isolation, the communities they live in also get affected, and in the long run, this loss is felt by the nation at large. When a person is unable to produce in whatever capacity, either in agriculture industry, or other forms of skilled labour, then certain sectors of the economy suffer.

HIV & AIDS, therefore, both infects people and affects those that interact with the infected persons from day to day. When a person is infected with AIDS, he or she ceases to contribute actively to community activities. Since many communities together form a nation, the effects of AIDS on an individual are finally translated into the effects on the country at large.

Many people who are dying of AIDS are young adults who have been educated using the country's resources. They are the ones working in key sectors, in the economy. If death due to HIV & AIDS continues unchecked, then the country will not have enough doctors, engineers, teachers, lawyers and other skilled workers necessary to manage the country's economy. In rural areas, the productive people who are involved in food production activities belong to the group that is at greatest risk of getting infected with the disease (KIE, 1999).

Everyone, irrespective of their sex, social status, race or age can get infected with the virus. However, infection and transmission of HIV & AIDS can be prevented. The hope for the control and spread of HIV & AIDS lies with the youth. This can be done by adopting the behaviour which will not lead to infection and spread the virus.

There is no cure for HIV & AIDS or any known vaccination against the virus. Because of this, the disease is dreaded in society. It is often associated with death and once people discover that they are infected, they become devastated. It is this devastation that causes the psychological problems facing persons infected with HIV & AIDS.

Persons infected with HIV, therefore, should not be subjected to cruel treatment, but should be handled with love, support and understanding.

### Interventions for Preventing the Transmission of HIV
The impact of AIDS may be very severe in Kenya if HIV infection continues to spread rapidly. However a number of interventions can slow the spread.

The major mode of transmission is through heterosexual contact and it is especially in this area that interventions have to be intensified. Interventions include promoting abstinence and faithfulness, promoting reduction in the number of sexual partners, encouraging delay in the onset of sexual activity among adolescents, promoting the correct use and consistent availability of condoms, strengthening programmes for STD control, and encouraging voluntary counselling and testing (MOH, 2001).

## Promoting Abstinence before Marriage and Faithfulness to One Partner

Abstinence and faithfulness can be promoted through a combination of mass media, counselling and education programmes. Delay in the onset of sexual activity among adolescents can have a significant impact on the spread of HIV. Information, education, communication and other programmes that address adolescents and the needs of young people are urgently needed. A reduction in HIV incidence (the annual rate of new infections) among today's young people would not only avoid much suffering but would also be a critical step in controlling the spread of the virus.

## Promoting Voluntary Counselling and Testing

In Voluntary Counselling and Testing (VCT) for HIV, a person receives the counselling needed to make an informed choice about whether to undergo confidential testing for HIV. The government of Kenya is fully committed to encouraging the provision of VCT services throughout Kenya so that all Kenyans who wish to know their HIV serostatus will have access to these services.

HIV Voluntary Counselling and Testing has been shown to have a role in both preventing HIV infection and, for people with the infection, as an entry point to care. It gives people an opportunity to learn to accept their HIV status in a confidential environment with counselling and referral for ongoing emotional support and medical care.

Pregnant women who are aware that they are HIV positive can prevent transmission to their infants. Knowledge of HIV status can also help people decide how to protect their sexual partners from infection if they are HIV positive. Studies have indicated that VCT can be a cost-effective intervention in preventing HIV transmission.

*Promoting the Use of and Availability of Condoms*
Another important intervention is to promote condom use through mass media, counselling and education and to increase the availability of condoms through expanded public distribution, social marketing programmes and programmes in the workplace. Special initiatives to promote condom use among high-risk populations (such as commercial sex workers and long distance truck drivers) have proven effective in some cases.

*Preventing Infection among Young People*
Levels of HIV infection are alarmingly high among young people, particularly young women. Special efforts are required to protect the youth. It is difficult to change any behaviour pattern, and especially sexual behaviour pattern. Around the world, successful prevention programmes among young people are those that equip adolescents with the knowledge, skills and attitudes that will keep them safe from infection before they become sexually active.

The government has recognized the vulnerability of youth. In Sessional Paper on AIDS in Kenya, it has committed itself to protecting young people from HIV infection by equipping them with adequate knowledge and skills. Further, the government has stated that, as a matter of policy, it has integrated AIDS education programmes into existing school curricula.

## Impact of HIV/AIDS on the Education Sector

The HIV & AIDS epidemic affects the education sector in at least three ways:
- Supply of experienced teachers is reduced by HIV & AIDS related illness and death;
- Children are kept out of School if they are needed at home, to care for sick family members or to work in the fields; and

- Children may drop out of school if their families cannot afford school fees due to reduced household income as a result of an HIV & AIDS death.

A special problem facing the education sector is that teenage children are especially susceptible to HIV infection. The sector faces a special challenge of educating this group to protect them.

Kenya has a literacy race of 76 per cent for females (NACC, 2000). Despite the advantages of these high literacy rates, the AIDS pandemic is threatening to reverse enrolment and completion rates. This will raise the proportion of vulnerable children and increase the incidence of child labour.

For many years there have been inadequacies in the Kenyan educational curricula which are generally not designed to discuss the many sensitive issues surrounding HIV & AIDS. Consequently, the introduction of essential family life skills has been inhibited or prohibited. However, the Ministry of Education through the Kenya Institute of Education has prepared an AIDS education syllabus for schools and colleges. It is now possible to teach AIDS education right from the primary schools through to college level.

The introduction of AIDS Education Syllabus for schools and colleges presents yet another milestone in education. It is a response to the challenges of HIV & AIDS prevention and control. The syllabus puts great emphasis on the need for behaviour development and change in order to combat the challenges posed by HIV & AIDS.

The AIDS education syllabus for schools prepared by the Kenya Institute of Education is divided into three sections: Primary school syllabus, Secondary school syllabus and Teachers Training College syllabus.

The purpose of the Secondary school AIDS curriculum, which happens to form the basis of this study, is to equip the students with the necessary knowledge, skills and attitudes that will enable them to adopt behaviour to help them take preventive measures against being infected with and spreading HIV & AIDS. In turn, it may be assumed that the students will communicate effectively, facts and issues on HIV & AIDS to their peers and other members of the society.

The syllabus aims at enriching the existing curriculum by focusing more on HIV & AIDS issues.

The education sector has the potential to influence behaviour formation and behaviour change among the youth. This sector is crucial in reaching out to almost 50 per cent of the population directly impacted on and engaged in the sector.

## NACC's Intervention and Policy Recommendations

The government through the National Aids Control Council has come up with a National HIV & AIDS Strategic Plan for the year 2000–2005. In this strategy, the government identifies the education sector to be a crucial one and therefore suggests several interventions and policy recommendations to forestall the impact of HIV/AIDS. Priority interventions in this sector include:

- Prevention and advocacy
- Enhanced community care for HIV & AIDS patients to avoid children being kept out of school to take care of sick relatives;
- Affirmative action by local community leaders, government, NGOs and local authorities in terms of school bursary funds.
- Better parenting of teenage children through inculcating in them good moral values. In addition, enhanced counselling of teenagers by religious leaders, and local leaders.
- Affirmative action to increase the girl child education. This is expected to prevent mother to child HIV & AIDS transmission through increased awareness;
- Using teachers as role models to sensitize school going children and the wider community on the dangers posed by HIV & AIDS pandemic;
- Counselling and sensitization of teaching fraternity, from college level to practising teachers;
- Better succession management in the education sector;

- Introducing family life education in schools to ensure sustainability of the strategic plan in the context of the education sectors.
- Enhanced resource mobilisation to cater for the wider school curricula, and;
- Research and development of Information and Education and Communication (IEC) and AIDS curricula in learning institutions.

### School Based Programs

There are a number of school-based programs that address HIV & AIDS to adolescents. The common approach to anti-AIDS programs to the youths has been either through a school curriculum or through activities organised through the school or through the community. School based programs include activities that are carried out as part of the curriculum, and informal activities that are carried out through voluntary involvement.

In June 2001 member states at the United Nations General Assembly Special Session on AIDS agreed to "ensure that by 2005, at least 90% of young men and women aged 15 to 24 have access to the information and education necessary to develop the life skill required to reduce their vulnerability to HIV infection." One way to achieve this goal, at least in theory, is through a country's education system – especially if the programs reach students at an early age, before some begin to drop out of school. At the International AIDS Conference in Durban in 2000, the "Prevention Works" Symposium recommended that HIV & AIDS education begin early, focusing on children as young as five years old.

### Kenya Institute of Education AIDS Education
### Project for the Youth

The Kenya Institute of Education (KIE) is charged with the mandate of developing school curriculum for Kenyan schools from primary school through to middle level colleges. There is a whole department in this unit that is devoted to HIV & AIDS, and STD curriculum development. HIV & AIDS, and STD curriculum is taught as part of the family life program that has been taught in schools since 1987. HIV & AIDS is dealt with as a communicable disease.

The most recent review of the curriculum has identified the need to strengthen its teaching and a proposal was developed and funding obtained from UNICEF. The main thrust has been to:

- Develop a comprehensive curriculum
- Develop student materials, and
- Train teachers

The current objectives are to expand and strengthen teaching of the HIV & AIDS curriculum. A life skills training approach has been adopted and inbuilt into this child-to-child approach. This method is cognisant of the reality that children need both knowledge and skills to achieve the goals of risk-free behaviour. The program also recognizes that children do not attend school or drop out and hence their school going peers are trained in child-to child activities so that they can reach their peers.

The curriculum was planned in 3 phases;

- Curriculum and materials development
- Teacher training, and
- Supervision and evaluation of the program.

A needs assessment was carried out in Nairobi, Kwale, Busia and Migori districts supported by the UNICEF. The results of this study have been used to develop materials and teachers manuals. The first phase has been completed. The second and third phases have not yet been implemented because of lack of funds. Funding and technical support was from UNICEF, Kenya country office.

Until recently, AIDS studies had been incorporated into the subjects of home Science, Religious studies and Geography, History and Civics.

The HIV & AIDS integrated curriculum is taught from Standard 1 in primary school throughout to the end of Secondary school. The new thrust in the curriculum has been to show teachers how they can integrate AIDS into all subjects, e.g. in maths. For example, AIDS data would be used when teaching bar charts. It has been hoped that in this approach, life skills are instilled in children. These skills include ability to make decisions, skills on the concept of building friendships and relationships, assertiveness, ability to think critically and skills on how to negotiate. Teachers will be trained on how to instil life skills and to recognize that children can be very effective peer educators.

Student materials have been developed and they promote interactive reading and learning. For example, in "Bloom or Doom: Your Choice," which is an AIDS resource book for Youth in and out of Secondary schools, there are case studies followed by questions and role plays, and teachers are encouraged to generate discussion among the students. The curriculum aims to equip the learner with knowledge about HIV & AIDS, and STDs, actions that can be taken to protect oneself from AIDS and how to support those affected by AIDS (KIE, 1999).

AIDS Education consists of knowledge, skills and attitudes meant to assist the learners to develop and adopt behaviour that will prevent them from being infected with HIV. It will also equip them with the necessary skills to pass on AIDS information to others, thereby helping them prevent HIV infection and control the spread of AIDS.

The major purpose of AIDS Education is behaviour development and change that is appropriate to the youth's stage of development that will help him (or her) in HIV & AIDS prevention and control.

## General Objectives

According to the HIV & AIDS curriculum (KIE), the learner should be able to:

- Acquire necessary knowledge, skills about HIV & AIDS, and STDs

- Appreciate facts and issues related to HIV & AIDS and STDs
- Develop life skills that will lead to AIDS and STDs free life
- Identify appropriate sources of information on HIV & AIDS related issues
- Make decisions about personal and social behaviour that reduce risk of HIV and STD's infection
- Show compassion towards and concern for those infected and affected by HIV & AIDS.
- Be actively involved in school and out of school activities aimed at prevention and control of HIV and STD's infections, and
- Communicate effectively with peers and others, issues and concerns related to HIV & AIDS and STD's.

The Secondary AIDS education syllabus deals with the subject matter in greater depth. The specific objectives are to be able to:

- Define the terms HIV & AIDS and STDs
- Explain the causes of AIDS and STDs
- Relate HIV infection to STDs and AIDS
- Explain the different ways of acquiring AIDS
- Know the ways AIDS is not transmitted
- Develop the habit of positive living as a group member
- State the different stages of HIV infection
- State ways of prevention and control of AIDS
- Develop the skills that will enable learners to decide and act in the prevention of HIV infection
- Explain the effects of AIDS in relation to family, community and the nation
- Identify beliefs and practices which promote or control the spread of HIV & AIDS
- Develop a sensitive attitude towards people with AIDS
- Describe ways of providing care and support to persons with AIDS, and

- Develop skills in caring and supporting persons infected and affected by AIDS.

In addition, the curriculum covers adolescent physical and psychological development and aims at developing skills among young people on how to be responsible, and to cope with these changes better. Religious and cultural values and their role in promoting or preventing AIDS are discussed in the context of learning how to relate appropriately to members of the opposite sex, and learning proper management of work and leisure time. The Secondary Schools AIDS Education Syllabus is taught in 78 lessons of 40 minutes each (52 hours).

Young people are highly vulnerable to HIV infection and should be the primary focus of communication strategy activities. Classrooms provide a great opportunity for the development of moral values since children are in their formative years and more readily able to absorb information on HIV & AIDS risk and to adopt safer attitudes and sexual practices.

Schools provide many opportunities for accurate and comprehensive HIV & AIDS education, behaviour development and values formation through life skills programme that teach negotiation and assertiveness. The Ministry of Education has commenced AIDS education in schools and although there are challenges, NACC has initiated a process to ensure that there is an appropriate range of communication materials to support these activities.

The capacity of teachers also needs to be addressed through training programmes and the provision of reference materials. Teacher training in any subject is important. For teaching information and skills related to reproductive health and HIV & AIDS, teacher training is even more essential and complex. In many countries of Sub-Saharan Africa, the AIDS epidemic has spread to the general population, with up to half of all new HIV infections occurring among the youth under age 25 (Tijuana, et al, 2004). Since most youth attend school at least for primary education, school-based programs are a logical place to reach young people. Understanding the importance and techniques of teacher training in sexuality education in Africa is particularly urgent.

The 2001 United Nations General Assembly Special Session on AIDS sought to ensure that by 2005, at least 90 percent of the world's youth have access to information and education necessary to reduce their vulnerability to AIDS (Tujuana et al, 2004). Teachers are a crucial link in providing valuable information about reproductive health and HIV & AIDS to youth. But to do so effectively, they need to understand the subject, acquire good teaching techniques, and understand what is developmentally and culturally appropriate. Teacher attitudes and experiences affect their comfort with, and capacity to teach about HIV & AIDS.

Teachers are often the main adults other than family members with whom young people interact on a daily basis. In an era of HIV & AIDS, teachers play an even more critical role of being a source of accurate information and a person with whom young people can raise sensitive and complicated issues about sexuality. As the AIDS epidemic spreads, the need becomes more urgent for teachers to discuss AIDS in the context of human development, sexuality and pregnancy prevention. Teachers also need to know how to protect their own health and the importance of not putting any of their students at risk through their own behaviours.

Ideally, as trusted gatekeepers of information, teachers may be instrumental in imparting knowledge and skills to young people. Teachers may function as role models, advocates for healthy school environments, guides for students in need of services, resources for accurate information, mentors and effective instructors. But to meet these expectations in the AIDS era, teachers may need skills and knowledge as well as support from the educational system and broader community.

The HIV & AIDS epidemic in developing countries has resulted in serious initiatives in revising educational curricula to integrate the HIV & AIDS component, and training teachers to use such curricula. All ministries of education are implementing one or more interventions to combat the epidemic in the education system (Akoulouze, et al; in Tijuana, et al, 2004).

Linkages between school programmes and community interventions around the schools are encouraged. HIV & AIDS communication may require being into extracurricular activities, parent and teacher associations and boards of governors' meetings (NACC, 2003).

The aim of this proposed study therefore is to evaluate the effectiveness of the school-based communication programme in the prevention of HIV & AIDS in adolescents. In this regard, the study focussed on HIV education programme in secondary schools.

In the following chapter I have offered a theoretical framework and a brief discussion of research methodology that I employed for the present study.

# CHAPTER THREE

# Theoretical Framework and Research Methodology

## Introduction

Having overviewed the current HIV & AIDS regime, I now proceed to offer a theoretical framework and a brief discussion of research methodology that I employed in the present study. I begin with some of the major theories that underlay my enquiry.

In the present study, I used three major communication theories. These were: Symbolic Interaction Theory, Diffusion Theory, and Cognitive Dissonance Theory. The basic aim of science is to find general explanations to natural events. According to Singleton (et al), 1988, all empirical studies should be grounded in theory. This means that they are conducted scientifically and can be empirically tested. Kerlinger et al (1964), define theory as "a set of interrelated concepts, definitions, and prepositions that present a systematic view of phenomenon by specifying relations among the variables with the purpose of explaining and predicting the phenomena". This means that the very nature of theory lies in its explanation of observed phenomena.

The use of theoretical models to address relevant HIV & AIDS issues in the Kenyan context requires careful consideration. This is because no one model adequately addresses the wide range of variables which inhibit or facilitate the behaviour change process. It is more likely that a combination of a number of these theoretical approaches will provide the optimum response for communications program planning in Kenya.

## Symbolic Interaction Theory

The basic premise of the above theory is that although people can learn through directly experiencing the consequences of their own behaviour, most human behaviour is learned observationally through modelling. From observing others, one forms an idea of how new behaviours are performed, and on later occasions this coded information serves as a guide for action.

The Symbolic Interaction theory postulates that most human behaviour is learned observationally through the informative function of modelling. Modelling is governed by the ability to observe the modelled activities, code them for memory-presentation, retain them, and match the modelled behaviour.

Social learning theory postulates behaviour as being regulated by the interplay of self-generated and external sources of influence. The theory recognizes that there is a continuous reciprocal interaction among person's behaviour, events going on inside the person (thoughts, emotional reactions, and expectations) and the environmental consequences of that behaviour.

From the social learning perspective, people, and students enact what they have learned.

## Diffusion Theory

One of the most important applications of mass communication research has been concerned with the process of encouraging the adoption of innovations. This is relevant both to developing and more advanced societies, since there is a continuing need, under conditions of social and technological change, to replace old methods by new techniques. It concerns mass communication, since there are many circumstances where potential changes originate in scientific research and public policy which, to be effective, have to be applied by many individuals or small organizations which are outside the direct centralized control of government or large undertakings (McQuail et al, 1981).

According to Rogers and Shoemaker's (1973) theory, the most important features about work on diffusion are: the weight which has been given to non-media (often personal) sources (neighbours, experts), the existence often of a campaign situation in which behavioural changes are sought by giving information and trying to influence motivations and attitudes.

The Diffusion Theory is based on the assumption that there are at least four distinct steps in an 'innovation diffusion' process.

- *Knowledge:* the individual is exposed to an awareness of the existence of the innovation and gains some understanding of how it works.
- *Persuasion:* the individual forms a favourable or unfavourable attitude towards the innovation.
- *Decision:* the individual engages in activities which lead to a choice to adopt or reject the innovation.
- *Confirmation:* the individual seeks reinforcement for the innovation decision he has made, but he may reverse his previous decision if exposed to conflicting messages about the innovation.

## Cognitive Dissonance Theory

Cognitive dissonance, also known as consistency theory, is one of the theories that have influenced the development of research on message reception and audience personalities. The others include learning theory and functional theory.

According to Tan (1985), the central thesis of dissonance theory is: we are rationalizing and not just rational animals, and that we react to messages mostly to justify or protect existing opinions, attitude and behaviours.

Dissonance theory was formulated by Festinger in 1957. According to Festinger, cognitive dissonance is aroused in an individual when two or more relevant cognitions simultaneously held by him or her contradict each other. Cognition is a thought about behaviour, an opinion, an attitude, or a choice. Cognitions contradict each other when logic, personal experience, established knowledge or other people imply that they are incompatible. An individual is therefore unable to justify the holding of two or more dissonant cognitions at the same time.

According to the Cognition Dissonance theory, dissonance is an uncomfortable drive state that can motivate the individual to action. Thus one in a dissonant state is primed for action. He or she will be motivated to do something to remove dissonance because it is psychologically uncomfortable.

Dissonance theory suggests not only that we will attempt to remove dissonance when it is present, but also that we will actively avoid its arousal. This is where selective exposure of information fits into the theory. Information contradicting existing attitudes, choices or behaviours can arouse dissonance, or maintain the desired consonant state, and should therefore be actively sought. The selective exposure hypothesis has two components:

(1) It predicts that we will actively avoid, or will be less receptive to information contradicting existing attitudes, behaviours and choices, and

(2) It predicts that we will seek out or be more receptive to supportive information.

Cognitive dissonance theory has been a useful guide in helping to explain human behaviour. It has helped to shed light on how people interact with each other in group settings and in one on one social interaction.

The relevance of this theory to my study was that if a student is forced to act or say something that is in conflict with his personal opinion, then he will feel a conflict between the opinion and action, and he will look for a way to reduce the amount of dissonance he or she feels. Generally, the person will change his opinion to match what he has said or acted out as the way of resolving this internal conflict. Also, the greater the amount of pressure is brought to an individual to induce a change of opinion, the more the tendency to change opinion is weakened.

Dissonance theory has made significant contribution to the field of attitude change. Its implications for the persuader are clear. High pressure tactics may get immediate compliance, but they won't get long term commitment. For example, adolescents with a history of having unprotected sex with multiple partners may admit they are at risk of HIV infection, but at the same time perceive that their careful selection of partners is an overriding preventive factor. The more people believe that an event can be controlled through personal actions, the greater the tendency to be optimistically biased in their judgements.

## Research Hypothesis

My hypothesis in the present study was:

HIV & AIDS education has raised the level of HIV & AIDS awareness, knowledge among    students in Kenya's Secondary schools.

## Research Methodology

Having briefly discussed the theoretical framework guiding the present study, I now proceed to describe the approaches and methods of my data collection, study site, sampling procedure, unit of analysis and data analysis.

## Unit of Analysis

These were the social entities whose social characteristics are the focus of this study. They were therefore the adolescents/students in Secondary schools who are being taught HIV & AIDS education.

## The Study Site

The present study was conducted in the Nairobi province. Nairobi was selected owing to its nearness to me at the time of undertaking the study and thus to help me to optimize my limited financial resources and time.

Nairobi has many public secondary schools which are located within the city and its outskirts. These allowed an easy access to me.

## Sampling Procedure

In order to collect representative information with acceptable accuracy and within the shortest time and limited resources, the study used purposive sampling technique. According to Mugenda et al (1999), purposive sampling "allows the researcher to use cases that have the required information with respect to the objectives of his or her study."

Simple random sampling was used as a criterion to select the students to be interviewed. A number was given to every student in a group. The numbers were then placed in a container and then picked at random. The students corresponding to the numbers picked were included in the sample. The sample size was 100 students.

## Methods of Data Collection

As I have already pointed out, the present study sought to evaluate the impact of the HIV & AIDS Education Programme in Kenya's Secondary Schools. Data for this study was derived from the Secondary school students, who are the respondents, and therefore the primary sources of information.

The survey method using the interview schedule was the only key research method used to extract data from the respondents. Primary data was derived from survey interviews with the respondents.

In the present study I used a questionnaire with structured or closed ended questions. The questions had a list of possible alternatives from which respondents selected the answer that best describes their situation. The questionnaires were self-administered.

## Data Analysis

According to Mugenda, et al, (1999), data analysis is the process of bringing order, structure and meaning to the mass of information collected.

Data was analysed according to the objectives of the study. The idea was to analyse data (information) in a systematic way in order to come to some useful conclusion and recommendations. Inferential statistics was used to infer sample results to the entire student population. Inferential statistics is concerned with determining how likely it is for the results obtained from a sample to be similar to results expected from the entire population.

In order to establish the impact of AIDS education percentages, graphs and pie-charts were used. The percentages were used to gauge the level of AIDS awareness among the sample size, and by extension, the greater student population in only the selected schools secondary schools.

## Limitations of the Study

The present study was marked by the following limitations:

- Lack of data about the HIV & AIDS prevalence among secondary school students at the time when HIV & AIDS education programme was being introduced in schools. As such, it was not possible to gauge whether, after the introduction of this HIV & AIDS education programme, the prevalence rates have increased or reduced. This then justified the research; to be able to generate the data that were missing.
- There was lack of information regarding the impact of the AIDS education programme which would have provided a perfect starting point.
- Limited funding was also a problem to carry out the entire survey.
- Time allocated for the study was short and this limited the depth of the study.
- Since all the questions were closed-ended, the possibility

that respondents may have given inaccurate responses cannot be ruled out.

My next chapter deals with data analysis.

# CHAPTER FOUR

# Results and Discussion

## Introduction

The purpose of chapter Four is to present results of the data analysis. Since the study is empirical in nature, statistics are used to summarise the results and to make deductions on the selected sample.

The title of the study was: *The Impact of HIV & AIDS Communication Strategies for Adolescents: A Case Study of HIV & AIDS Education Programme in Kenya's Secondary Schools.* The study had one objective, which was, to investigate the levels of awareness, knowledge and information that the youth have gained through this education programme.

The study had one hypothesis: HIV & AIDS education has raised the level of HIV & AIDS awareness, knowledge among students in Kenyan Secondary schools. The impact was measured by measuring awareness.

The data has been analysed according to the objectives of the study. The purpose of doing this is to come up with some useful conclusion and recommendations.

## Respondents

One hundred (100) respondents were interviewed within Nairobi Province. The total population of the schools was 550 students. Only students in form four were sampled. The selection criterion is explained in chapter three. East lands area was the focus of the study. The choice of east lands was informed by its proximity to the researcher. 10 schools from this area were chosen for the study.

Sixty (60) respondents were male while 40 were female, representing 60% and 40% respectively of the total respondents. The respondents were aged between 15 and 18 years.

Distribution of respondents by sex

| Sex | Percent |
|---|---|
| Male | 60 |
| Female | 40 |
| **TOTAL** | **100** |

## Data Analysis and Interpretation

*Knowledge of HIV*

The results are indicated in the following pie-charts.

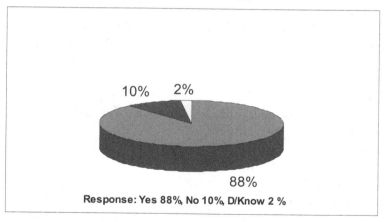

Response: Yes 88%, No 10%, D/Know 2 %

The author sought to find out if the students knew what HIV stands for. This is because the course content provided that students understand the meaning of HIV and AIDS. This knowledge was necessary since it formed the basis of the discussion.

In the above results, 88 respondents said that they know what HIV stands for. 10 respondents said that they didn't know what HIV stands for. Another 2 respondents indicated that they did not know what HIV stands for.

*Knowledge of AIDS*

| Response | Frequency | Percent |
|---|---|---|
| Yes | 91 | 91 |
| No | 7 | 7 |
| Don't Know | 2 | 2 |
| **TOTAL** | **100** | **100** |

The results are indicated in the following pie-chart.
Majority of the students interviewed (91%) agreed that they knew

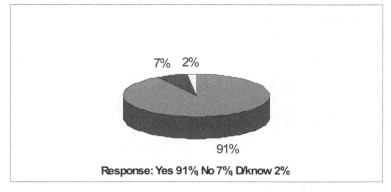

7%   2%

91%

Response: Yes 91% No 7% D/know 2%

what AIDS stands for. Seven percent students said they did not know while 2 students had nothing to say about the question. These results attest to the fact that the expected outcome from the course in getting to know what AIDS stands for was realised.

*Does HIV Cause AIDS?*
The respondents were the asked if HIV causes AIDS. This was necessary to know because the connection between the two variables needs to be established. The course teaches that HIV causes AIDS. It was therefore necessary to establish whether this awareness had been created.

| Response | Frequency | Percent |
|---|---|---|
| Yes | 86 | 86 |
| No | 10 | 10 |
| Don't Know | 4 | 4 |
| **TOTAL** | **100** | **100** |

The results are presented in the following bar graph.
From the above results, majority of the respondents, 86 indicated

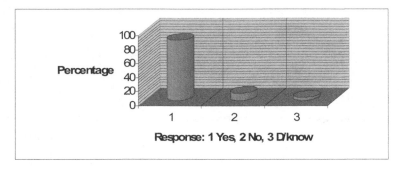

they know that HIV causes AIDS. Ten percent students indicated that HIV does not cause AIDS while only 4 students didn't know whether HIV causes AIDS or not. The results mean that the course content, particularly the section dealing with HIV and AIDS, had been understood by the respondents.

*AIDS Weakens the Body's Immune System*
When asked if AIDS weakens the body's immune system, most respondents, as shown below responded in the affirmative.

| Response | Frequency | Percent |
|----------|-----------|---------|
| True | 90 | 90 |
| False | 5 | 5 |
| Dont Know | 5 | 5 |
| **TOTAL** | **100** | **100** |

The above results are presented in the following bar graph.

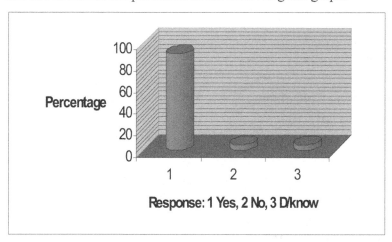

The above results indicate that 90 students agreed that AIDS weakens the body's immune system. Five percent students disagreed while 5 others had no say, they didn't know whether AIDS weakens the body's immune system or not. This is an indication that the course had created awareness to the respondents.

The respondents were asked whether they knew that AIDS is transmitted sexually. Majority of the respondents were aware as the results below indicate.

*Sexual intercourse can transmit AIDS*

| Response | Frequency | Percent |
|----------|-----------|---------|
| True | 96 | 96 |
| False | 3 | 3 |
| Don't Know | 1 | 1 |
| **TOTAL** | **100** | **100** |

The above results are presented in the following bar graph.

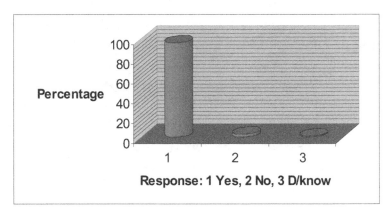

From the results, majority of the respondents (96%) agreed that AIDS is also transmitted sexually. Three percent students disagreed with the statement, while 1 student had no idea. The results give a clear indication that the respondents were aware that sexual relations are a precursor to AIDS related ailments. This is knowledge that may be used to challenge participants to consider safe sex practices or total abstinence altogether.

*HIV virus can be transmitted to other persons*

| Response | Frequency | Percent |
|---|---|---|
| True | 98 | 98 |
| False | 1 | 1 |
| Don't Know | 1 | 1 |
| **TOTAL** | **100** | **100** |

The above results are presented in the following pie-chart

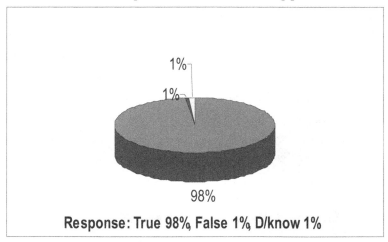

1%
1%
98%
**Response: True 98% False 1% D/know 1%**

A great majority of the students, 98 agreed that an HIV infected person can transmit the virus to another person. Only 1 student disagreed with the statement and another 1 student didn't have an answer. This level of awareness is necessary if the spread of the disease is to kept at bay.

*Blood that has the HIV virus causes AIDS*

| Response | Frequency | Percent |
|----------|-----------|---------|
| True | 96 | 96 |
| False | 3 | 3 |
| Don't Know | 1 | 1 |
| **TOTAL** | **100** | **100** |

These results are presented in the following pie chart

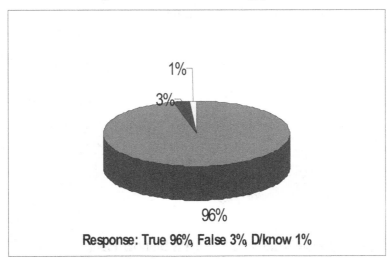

Response: True 96%, False 3%, D/know 1%

A big number of respondents, 96 per cent, agreed that anyone receiving blood that has HIV virus can get AIDS. 3 respondents disagreed with the statement while 1 respondent didn't have any answer. This is indicates that the respondents are aware that contaminated blood is in a position to transmit AIDS. This knowledge is essential for any necessary precautions to be taken by the students.

*Unsterilized skin piercing instruments transmit the HIV virus*

| Response | Frequency | Percent |
|----------|-----------|---------|
| Yes | 91 | 91 |
| No | 8 | 8 |
| Don't Know | 1 | 1 |
| **TOTAL** | **100** | **100** |

The above results are presented in the bar graph below

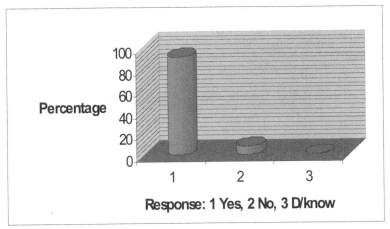

When asked whether sharing unsterilized skin piercing instruments can transmit the virus to the next user, 91 respondents agreed. 8 other disagreed and 1 respondent didn't know. This knowledge is necessary because it will help people to make the right choices.

*Mothers can infect their new borns with HIV during birth*

| Response | Frequency | Percent |
|----------|-----------|---------|
| Yes | 96 | 96 |
| No | 3 | 3 |
| Don't Know | 1 | 1 |
| **TOTAL** | **100** | **100** |

The above results are presented in the following bar graph

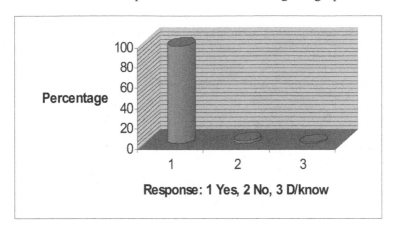

Majority of the students (96%) agreed that mothers can infect their new borns with HIV during birth. Another 3% disagreed with the statement, while 1 student didn't have any answer. It is therefore important that the right procedures and or attention be given to mothers during delivery.

*Vaginal secretions/fluids contain AIDS virus*

| Response | Frequency | Percent |
|---|---|---|
| Yes | 96 | 96 |
| No | 3 | 3 |
| Don't Know | 1 | 1 |
| **TOTAL** | **100** | **100** |

The above results are presented in the bar graph below

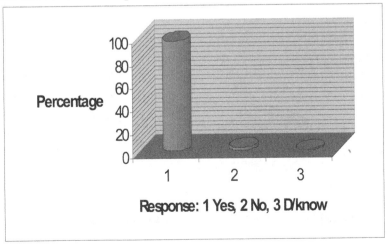

From the above results, 84 students agreed that vaginal secretions/ fluids can contain the AIDS virus. 8 students disagreed while another 8 didn't know what answer to give. Armed with this information, students can take the necessary precautions to avoid any contact with vaginal fluids.

*There is a relationship between weight loss and AIDS*
This question returned very interesting views from the respondents as shown below.

| Response | Frequency | Percent |
|---|---|---|
| True | 45 | 45 |
| False | 50 | 50 |
| Don't Know | 5 | 5 |
| **TOTAL** | **100** | **100** |

The above results are presented in the following pie chart

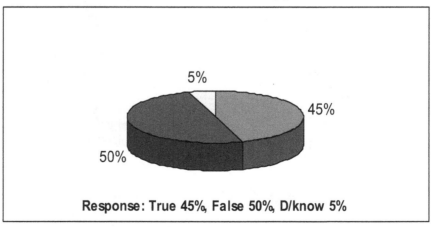

Response: True 45%, False 50%, D/know 5%

Half the students in the sample do not believe that loss of body weight within a very short time is a major sign of AIDS. Only 45 students believe the statement is true. 5 others had no idea what to say. These results confirm the view held by most people; that weight loss is not an indication that one has AIDS. It is true that losing weight doesn't have to indicate the presence of HIV, but the opposite can also be true.

*The surest way to know about one's HIV status is take an HIV test*

| Response | Frequency | Percent |
|----------|-----------|---------|
| True | 90 | 90 |
| False | 7 | 7 |
| Don't Know | 3 | 3 |
| **TOTAL** | **100** | **100** |

The above results are presented in a pie-chart below

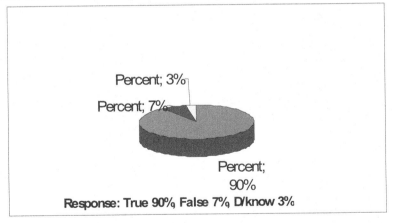

Percent; 3%

Percent; 7%

Percent; 90%

Response: True 90% False 7% D/know 3%

Majority of the respondents, 90 were in agreement that a blood test is a sure way of getting to know one's HIV status. 7 respondents disagreed with the statement while 3 had no answer. This result confirms the importance of every one taking an HIV test. This will enable such persons to plan their lives and even live responsibly.

*Can AIDS be cured?*

| Response | Frequency | Percent |
|----------|-----------|---------|
| Yes | 8 | 8 |
| No | 90 | 90 |
| Don't Know | 2 | 2 |
| **TOTAL** | **100** | **100** |

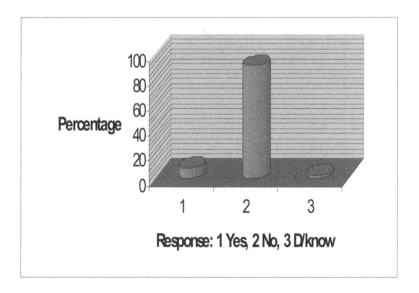

In a bar graph, the results are as follows.

Most students know that AIDS cannot be cured. Only 8 students think AIDS can be cured. Another 2 did not know what to say. It is important when majority of the students know that there is no cure for HIV & AIDS. This awareness will help them to appreciate good behaviour in the knowledge that there is no remedy for their wayward mannerisms.

*Sexually transmitted infections increase the chances of contracting HIV & AIDS*

When the students were asked if sexually transmitted infections increases the chances of contracting HIV & AIDS, they gave the following responses.

| Response | Frequency | Percent |
|----------|-----------|---------|
| True | 85 | 85 |
| False | 10 | 10 |
| Don't Know | 5 | 5 |
| **TOTAL** | **100** | **100** |

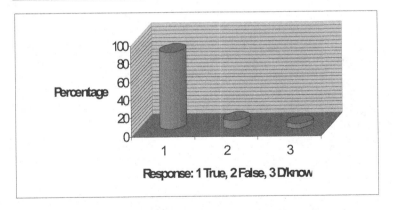

Response: 1 True, 2 False, 3 D/know

The above results are presented in a bar graph below

Majority of the respondents agreed with the statement that sexually transmitted infections increase the chance of contracting HIV & AIDS. Only 10 disagreed with the statement and 5 did not support or disagree. They didn't know the answer. There is no doubt that students should take every precaution to not only stay free from HIV & AIDS but also from sexually transmitted diseases. This is because HIV & AIDS thrives best in an environment of STDs.

*Pre-marital Sex and HIV & AIDS*
The students were equally asked if pre-marital sex increases the chances of contracting HIV & AIDS. Their responses are given below.

| Response | Frequency | Percent |
|----------|-----------|---------|
| True | 89 | 89 |
| False | 8 | 8 |
| Don't Know | 3 | 3 |
| **TOTAL** | **100** | **100** |

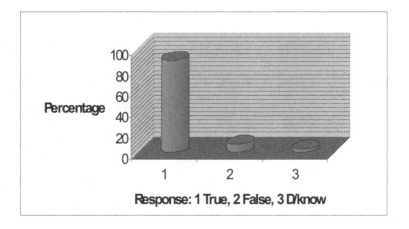

The above results are presented in the bar graph below
Most agreed that pre-marital sex increases the chances of contracting HIV & AIDS. Another 8 students disagreed with the statement while only 3 indicated that they did not know whether the statement is true or not. It is encouraging to note that students know the dangers of pre-marital sex. Such awareness should enable them to take the necessary steps in trying to keep themselves away from activities that expose them to the dangers that they already know.

*People infected with HIV & AIDS should be assisted to live comfortably*
There was a general feeling that those people living with HIV & AIDS should be assisted in order to live meaningful lives.

| Response | Frequency | Percent |
|---|---|---|
| Yes | 95 | 95 |
| No | 1 | 1 |
| Don't Know | 4 | 4 |
| **TOTAL** | **100** | **100** |

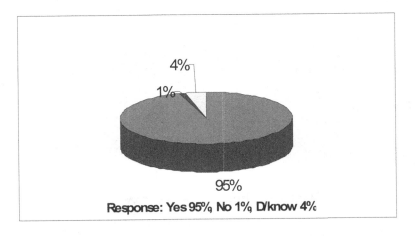

95%

Response: Yes 95% No 1% D/know 4%

The above results are presented in a pie chart below
Majority of the students were in agreement that people living with
HIV and AIDS should be assisted to live meaningful lives with their
families and within the community. Only 1 student disagreed. 4
students did not know. This is an encouraging reaction coming from
the students. If the war on HIV & AIDS stigma is to be won, then
all and sundry must take up this war. All forms and manner of discrimination should be avoided at all costs. By so doing, we will be
half way in fighting the spread of the scourge.

*Girls reach adolescence between ages twelve and eighteen*
As indicated below, there were mixed reactions to this question.

| Response | Frequency | Percent |
|---|---|---|
| True | 75 | 75 |
| False | 20 | 20 |
| Don't Know | 5 | 5 |
| **TOTAL** | **100** | **100** |

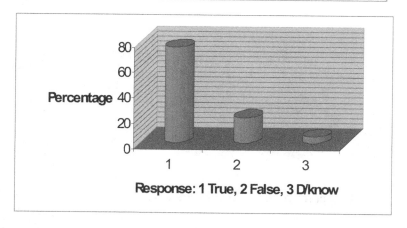

The above results are presented in the following bar graph
Majority of the respondents agreed that girls reach adolescence when
they are between the ages of 12 and 18. 20 of the 100 interviewed
disagreed with the statement. A further 5 didn't know what to say.
This response shows the need for girls to begin to understand their
bodies and the changes that go with them early so that they can take
the necessary precautions as they relate with boys.

*Many adolescents become victims of HIV & AIDS because of
irresponsible behaviour*

| Response | Frequency | Percent |
|----------|-----------|---------|
| True | 92 | 92 |
| False | 7 | 7 |
| Don't Know | 1 | 1 |
| **TOTAL** | **100** | **100** |

The above results are presented in a bar graph below

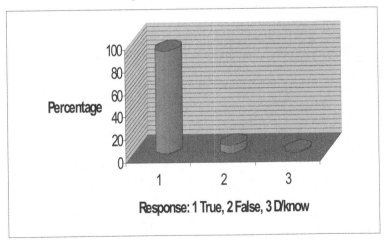

Response: 1 True, 2 False, 3 D/know

Majority of the respondents agreed that many adolescents become victims of HIV & AIDS because of irresponsible behaviour. 7 others disagreed with the statement while only 1 respondent didn't know what to say. This response is very helpful because young people can take responsibility for their actions. There is need for parents, teachers and other stakeholders to bear in mind that they can assist adolescents at this stage of their growth to keep off high risk behaviours that threaten their health.

*Can sexual intimacy make one contract HIV & AIDS?*
Majority of the respondents were in agreement that sexual intimacy can lead to contracting this deadly disease. The responses given are analysed below.

| Response | Frequency | Percent |
|----------|-----------|---------|
| True | 89 | 89 |
| False | 10 | 10 |
| Don't Know | 1 | 1 |
| **TOTAL** | **100** | **100** |

The above results have been presented in the following bar graph

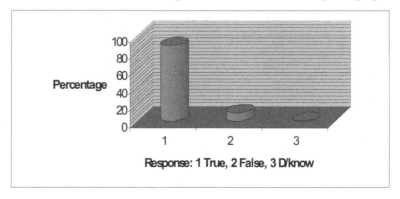

Majority of the respondents agreed that sexual intimacy can make one contract HIV & AIDS. 10 others disagreed while 1 respondent didn't have an answer. Unprotected sexual intimacy can lead to HIV & AIDS. Further, care must be taken by all to stay away from illicit relationships that not only pose a risk of contracting HIV & AIDS but also other infectious ailments.

*The youth must take responsibility to protect themselves against possible sexual dangers*
When asked if they took responsibility to protect themselves, most respondents agreed.

| Response | Frequency | Percent |
|----------|-----------|---------|
| True | 96 | 96 |
| False | 2 | 2 |
| Don't Know | 2 | 2 |
| **TOTAL** | **100** | **100** |

These results are presented below in a pie chart

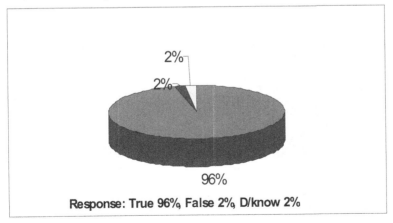

2%
2%
96%
Response: True 96%, False 2%, D/know 2%

The majority of respondents agreed that the youth must take re-sponsibility to protect themselves against possible sexual dangers. Only 2 respondents disagreed while a similar number (2) didn't have an answer. There is need for all players in the area of health to appreciate the fact that young people have a role to play in trying to protect themselves. All support due to them in this regard should be given them.

*Do you think AIDS education is an important aspect of our culture?* Almost all the respondents were in agreement that AIDS education is necessary to all.

| Response | Frequency | Percent |
|---|---|---|
| Yes | 98 | 98 |
| No | 1 | 1 |
| Don't Know | 1 | 1 |
| **TOTAL** | **100** | **100** |

The above results are presented in a pie chart

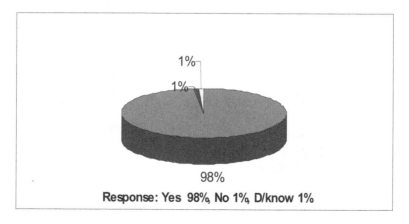

1%
1%
98%
**Response: Yes 98%, No 1%, D/know 1%**

Most respondents agreed that AIDS education is an important aspect of our culture. Only 1 respondent disagreed and a similar number didn't know. This is an important development given that in most of our cultures, sex and others related matters are a taboo to talk about openly. It therefore helps to teach AIDS education in schools so that students can benefit from such information and by so doing be able to make informed decisions in life. This is why most of the respondents interviewed supported the idea that AIDS education continues to be taught in schools.

# CHAPTER FIVE

# Summary, Conclusions, and Recommendations

## Summary

One of the national goals of education in Kenya is individual development and self-fulfilment (KIE, 1999). Education should provide opportunities for the fullest development of individual talents and personality. It should help children to develop their potential interest and abilities. A vital aspect of individual development is character building. Education should foster sound morals and religious values in order to help children grow up into self-disciplined, self reliant and integrated citizens.

The purpose of this study was to evaluate the impact of the AIDS education programme in Secondary schools in Kenya. The introduction of this AIDS education in schools by the government was meant to be a response to the challenges of HIV & AIDS prevention and control. The AIDS education syllabus for schools, for example, puts great emphasis on the need for behaviour development and change in order to combat the challenges posed by HIV & AIDS.

In order to facilitate my evaluation, I designed and personally administered a questionnaire. The questionnaire contained thirty (30) close-ended questions. A total of 100 students were selected to fill a questionnaire each. Only students in public schools in Nairobi Province were selected to provide answers to the questions asked. These questions were formulated to broadly cover all the areas that the AIDS syllabus seeks to cover from form one to form four. I assumed that teachers followed this syllabus alongside other teaching resources and aids. I further assumed that ultimately, the learners are supposed to know all that appertains to HIV & AIDS, responsible behaviour, signs and symptoms of AIDS, youth and sexuality, effects of HIV & AIDS on the individual, family, community and the nation and the care and support of people living with HIV & AIDS.

The data collected from the field using the questionnaire was first put together by tallying. The reason here was to get the exact number of respondents for each question asked or statement made. There were five choices of responses, which the respondents had to use to answer their questions. These were Yes, No, True, False, Don't know. With the number of respondents in each category, it was now possible to get a percentage score for the responses given against each question or statement.

One of the major findings of this study was that majority of the respondents interviewed indicated that they have learned much from AIDS education. From the answers given, I concluded that students in the selected secondary schools under investigation virtually know all aspects or issues related to HIV & AIDS, specifically the issues they study in school. Majority of those interviewed returned a right answer to the questions asked and or statements made based on the AIDS syllabus.

## Conclusion

Based on the objective of this study, which was to investigate the levels of awareness, knowledge and information the youth have gained through AIDS education, the present study concludes that since its inception communication strategies in HIV & AIDS education have had a tremendous impact with regard to what it was set out to achieve. The high number of respondents who have given the right answers as required is very encouraging.

The above conclusion means that there is a connection between awareness and education. HIV & AIDS education has raised awareness about HIV & AIDS. This is evidenced by the findings from the study. There is also a link between education and the knowledge about HIV & AIDS, and the results of the study testify to this.

However, from the study, there are those who indicated in their answers that they either did not agree or didn't know anything concerning what was being stated. Such students cannot be overlooked. They represent those in the system or in the entire population whose levels of awareness or knowledge have not been increased by AIDS education. Teachers have a responsibility to teach such students so that they grasp the basics and ideas of AIDS content. It is for their own good and advantage.

## Recommendations

The communication needs of Kenyan adolescents can best be analysed and understood in the context of special characteristics of these adolescents, the challenges that they face in life, and the dynamics that are normally associated with the adolescents. It should be noted that effective communication for the youth such as behaviour and attitude change is necessary if HIV campaign activities are to achieve the desired results.

The youth in Kenya have unique communication needs derived from their special and dynamic realities. While attempting to understand the communication needs of the youth in Kenya, it should be appreciated that the adolescent is a product of diverse socio-cultural backgrounds and economic lifestyles, which collectively impact on the communication needs.

Communication strategies and efforts need not be uniform and standardised, since the youth themselves are not homogeneous. Thus, the challenge lies in the search for a common denominator that addresses the needs and aspirations of Kenyan youth while designing the Information, Education and Communication (IEC), targeting them on HIV & AIDS and sexuality.

When designing effective communication strategies for the youth on HIV & AIDS, there's a need to understand the needs and motivations of this group, such as their hopes, dreams and aspirations. It's important to understand the young person through the leisure activities that they pursue, including fun activities indulged in, media preferences, how they relate to advertising, common language among youth and their views on sexuality.

Based on the study findings, a number of recommendations can be made:

- Schools should be more proactive in addressing sexuality, HIV & AIDS. It is recommended that the study of sexuality and HIV and AIDS be adequately addressed within the HIV & AIDS curriculum at the school level.
- Trained educators and counsellors should be used to handle the subject of HIV & AIDS and ensure the privacy that is needed when discussing sexuality.
- Even though the rate of awareness on HIV & AIDS is high, the study recommends that adolescents require more information on all aspects of HIV & AIDS, skills of protecting themselves from HIV infection, resisting peer pressure, being assertive and negotiating for safer sex.
- With regard to sexuality, the study recommends that information on the rapid sexual and physiological development be communicated to the adolescents. It is also recommended that information on reproductive health, pregnancy, contraception and male-female relationships be made available in order to prepare them to face the adolescence crisis.
- There is need for the government to include a chapter on contraceptives. The syllabus is silent on the contentious issue of condoms, for instance. Does it mean that such a discussion in schools is unwarranted?
- There is need for the government through the Ministry of Education to keep up-to-date records of those students that have in the past been infected by and or died of HIV & AIDS. Other than the results of the Demographic Health Survey (DHS) of 2003, which do not have any figures of

AIDS related infections for high school students, no reference materials are available elsewhere.

- The National AIDS Control Council (NACC) should work closely with the Kenya Institute of Education (KIE) to prepare more teaching aids for this programme. Interestingly, only one resource material, *"Bloom or Doom: Your Choice"* by KIE is being used in secondary schools to teach AIDS syllabus. This is hardly sufficient. More teaching aids and resources are needed.

The study and its findings are by no means exhaustive. It has opened many avenues for research and experimentation. Future studies should have a larger sample from diverse areas of the country other than Nairobi. Such studies will perhaps unearth findings different from the ones in this study. Further, studies could be conducted to find out whether the rates of HIV & AIDS infection among students, if any, are low or high with this knowledge and information about HIV & AIDS.

*HIV & AIDS, Communication, and Secondary Education in Kenya*

# APPENDIX ONE

Regards,

I am pursuing a Master of Arts in Communication Studies at the University of Nairobi. Currently, I am doing a study on the impact of the AIDS Education Programme in Secondary Schools as part of my dissertation.

Kindly feel free to provide the required information.

NB: DO NOT write your name anywhere in the questionnaire.

Thanks in advance for your assistance.

Faithfully,

**<u>NDETI NDATI</u>**

# APPENDIX TWO

## A Questionnaire on the Impact of the AIDS Education Programme in Secondary Schools

Please answer the following questions by ticking against the answer you think is appropriate.

1. Do you know what HIV stands for?

   Yes ☐

   No ☐

   Don't know ☐

2. Do you know what AIDS stands for?

   Yes ☐

   No ☐

   Don't know ☐

3. Does HIV cause AIDS?

   Yes ☐

   No ☐

   Don't know ☐

4. AIDS weakens the body's immune system.

True ☐

False ☐

Don't know ☐

5. AIDS is also transmitted sexually.

True ☐

False ☐

Don't know ☐

6. When a person has HIV & AIDS, he/she can transmit the virus to another person.

True ☐

False ☐

Don't know ☐

7. If you receive blood that has HIV virus then you will get AIDS.

True ☐

False ☐

Don't know ☐

8. Can sharing unsterilized skin piercing instruments transmit t
   virus from an  infected person to the next user?

   Yes

   No

   Don't know


9. Mothers can infect their new borns with HIV during birth.

   Yes

   No

   Don't know


10. Can vaginal secretions/fluids contain the AIDS virus?

    Yes

    No

    Don't know


11. Semen contains AIDS virus.

    Yes

    No

    Don't know

12. Loss of body weight within a very short time is a major sign of AIDS.

   True ☐

   False ☐

   Don't know ☐

13. The surest way to know about one's HIV status is to take an HIV blood test.

   True ☐

   False ☐

   Don't know ☐

14. Can AIDS be cured?

   Yes ☐

   No ☐

   Don't know ☐

15. Sexually transmitted infections increase the chance of one contracting HIV & AIDS.

   True ☐

   False ☐

   Don't know ☐

16. Pre-marital sex increases the chances of contracting HIV & AIDS.

True ☐

False ☐

Don't know ☐

17. Blood for transfusion should be screened before being used.

True ☐

False ☐

Don't know ☐

18. Should people infected with HIV & AIDS be assisted to live meaningful lives within the community and with their families.

Yes ☐

No ☐

Don't know ☐

19. Does eating a balanced diet help an HIV infected person live longer?

Yes ☐

No ☐

Don't know ☐

20. Girls reach adolescence between ages twelve and eighteen.

True ☐

False ☐

Don't know ☐

21. Boys reach adolescence between ages fourteen to twenty.

True ☐

False ☐

Don't know ☐

22. Our feelings and attitudes during adolescence make us behave and react in certain ways as we interact with members of the society.

True ☐

False ☐

Don't know ☐

23. Many adolescents become victims of HIV & AIDS because of irresponsible behaviour.

True ☐

False ☐

Don't know ☐

24. Can sexual intimacy make one contract HIV & AIDS.

Yes ☐

No ☐

Don't know ☐

25. The youth must take responsibility to protect themselves against possible sexual dangers.

True ☐

False ☐

Don't know ☐

26. Do you think AIDS education is an important aspect of our culture?

Yes ☐

No ☐

Don't know ☐

27. The effects of HIV & AIDS can be translated from the family to the community.

True ☐

False ☐

Don't know ☐

28. There has been a steady increase of AIDS orphans in Kenyan families.

True ☐

False ☐

Don't know ☐

29. AIDS epidemic has had far reaching negative effects on all the Sectors of the economy.

True ☐

False ☐

Don't know ☐

30. Should AIDS education continue being taught in schools?

Yes ☐

No ☐

Don't know ☐

*HIV & AIDS, Communication, and Secondary Education in Kenya*

# BIBLIOGRAPHY

AIDSCAP, *AIDS in Kenya: Socioeconomic Impact and Policy Implications*, USA, 1996.

AIDSCAP, *How to Create an Effective Communication Project,* Family Health International, USA.

Alexis Tan, 2nd Edition; *Mass Communication Theories and Research,* John Wiley and Sons, Inc., 1985.

CBS, *Kenya Demographic & Health Survey, 2003,* Preliminary Report, Nairobi, Kenya.

Kiai, W. in AAWORD, *Gender and HIV/AIDS in Africa,* AAWORD Publications, Senegal, 2003.

GOK, National Development Plan, 2002-2008, *Effective Management for sustainable Economic Growth & Poverty Reduction.*

Julia, Beamish, 2002, *Reporting on HIV/AIDS in Africa: A manual.*

KIE, *AIDS Education Syllabus for schools and Colleges,* 1999.

KIE, *Bloom or Doom: Your Choice, An AIDS Resource Book for youth in and out of Secondary Schools,* 1999.

McQuail, D., et al, *Communication Models, for the Study of Mass Communications,* Longman Inc, New York, 1981.

MOH, *Contraceptive Commodities,* Procurement Plan, 2003 – 2006, 203.

Moemeka, A. in Charles Okigbo, *Development Communication Principles,* ACCE, Nairobi, 1996.

MOH, *Homecare Handbook,* Reference Manual for Home-Based Care for People Living with HIV/AIDS in Kenya, 2002.

Mugenda, O. M. and Mugenda, A. G., *Research Methods, Qualitative and Quantitative Approaches*: Nairobi, Acts Press, 1991.

NACC, *A National HIV/AIDS Communication Strategy for Kenya*, Draft Strategy, 2001.

NACC, *AIDS in Kenya* 6th Edition, Background, Projections, Impact, Interventions and Policy, 2001.

NACC, *Kenya National HIV/AIDS Communication Strategy, 2002 – 2005*, August 2003.

NACC, *Kenya National HIV/AIDS Strategic Plan, 2000 – 2005*, 2000.

NACC, *Mainstreaming Gender into the Kenya National HIV/ AIDS Strategic Plan, 2000 – 2005*, 2002.

NACC, *National Programme Guidelines on Orphans and Other Children Made Vulnerable by HIV/AIDS*, 2003.

National Aids Control Programme, 2001, *Report of the National Status of AIDS in Kenya*; Nairobi.

Nduati, R. and Wambui K., 1996, *Communicating with Adolescents on HIV/AIDS in East Southern Africa*, Regal Press Kenya Ltd, Nairobi

Panos Report, No. 254, December, 2003

Tijuana A. James – Traore, William Finger, *Teacher Training: Essential for School – Based Reproductive Health and HIV/ AIDS Education*, Family Health International, Youth Net Programmes USA 2004.

UNESCO, *Media and HIV/AIDS in East Africa and Southern Africa: A Resource Book*, 2000.

World Bank Institute, Development Outreach, Vol. 6, No. 2, 2004.

## Zapf Chancery Tertiary Level Publications Continuation

*An Introduction to Philosophy of Religion* by **John M. M. Kasyoka (2008)**

*Pastoral Theology: Rediscovering African Models and Methods* by **John Ndung'u Ikenye (2009)**

*The Royal Son: Balancing Barthian and African Christologies* by **Zablon Bundi Mutongu (2009)**

*AIDS, Sexuality, and Gender: Experiences of Women in Kenyan Universities* by **Nyokabi Kamau (2009)**

*Modern Facilitation and Training Methodology: A Guide to Best Practice in Africa* by **Frederick K.Chelule (2009)**

*How to Write a Winning Thesis: Illustrated from an Actual Thesis* by **Kang'ethe et al (2009)**

*Absolute Power and other stories* by **Ambrose Keitany (2009)**

*Y'sdom in Africa: A Personal Journey* by **Stanley Kinyeki (2010)**

*Abortion and Morality Debate in the African Context* by **George Kegode (2010)**

*The Holy Spirit as Liberaotor* by **Joseph Koech (2010)**

*Modeling Servant-Leaders for Africa: Lessons from St. Paul* by **Ndung'u John Brown Ikenye (2010)**

*Biblical Studies, Theology, Religion and Philosophy: An Introduction for African Universities,* General Editor: **James N. Amanze (2010)**